phac
5/17

Blue Tarp

poems by

Rachel Joy Watson

Finishing Line Press
Georgetown, Kentucky

Blue Tarp

ACKNOWLEDGMENTS

"Salinas," "You Left," "What We Know in Part," and "Catching Lizards in
Summer" first appeared in *Cordella Magazine, Issue Five*.

"Autobiography" was published in *Literary Juice* in May of 2016.

I have to thank my dear friend Josh Giddens for finding something good in
every poem I write and for signing me up to perform at that poetry slam in
Tulsa all those years ago. It was a game changer. Thank you, Cate (of *Cordella
Magazine*) for being the first to publish my poetry. And to my students, thank
you for making me a better poet. You are the bravest writers I know.

Publisher: Leah Maines

Editor: Christen Kincaid

Cover Art: Jordan Armstrong

Author Photo: Janice Thompson

Cover Design: Elizabeth Maines

Printed in the USA on acid-free paper.
Order online: www.finishinglinepress.com
also available on amazon.com

Author inquiries and mail orders:
Finishing Line Press
P. O. Box 1626
Georgetown, Kentucky 40324
U. S. A.

Table of Contents

Autobiography

I'm like one of those toy boats that never made it out to sea,
just got pushed over dirt and rocks
and across the living room carpet

by a boy
with a keen imagination.

Song of Innocence

On the first day of summer
we take off our shoes,
find the sharpest rocks in the yard,
and walk over them again and again
until the calluses build up under our feet.
Every cringe is worth it because
by the end of summer
we can walk anywhere without pain.
It's hot and dry, so we beg mom to drive us to the beach.
She does, every day
until she finally gets fed up with the price of sunscreen
and the sand we drag into the car, so
she bans us from asking.
We dig a hole in the backyard,
cover it with a blue tarp,
turn the hose on and fill it up.
Mom watches from inside as we
jump into our homemade swimming pool
made up of 50% mud, 50% water.
As the day cools off we
turn over rocks in search of bugs,
make arrowheads out of clay gravel,
climb young trees that bend and sway
as we tackle them to test their strength—
to test our strength.

Summer is our season.

My Life (With You)

I wanted to finish something I started.
So when we kissed that first time
and you said, *we can do better*

I thought,
*let's make this homework
for the rest of our lives.*

I want to make plans for the future.
I want to live inside a giant bookshelf
disguised as a house.
I want a vegetable and herb garden out back,
cornflowers unbinding their roots
in a claw-foot tub,
easy access to my easy-bake-oven,
finger paintings hung like sconces on the wall,
and you
in a chair
studying,
thinking,
reading,
dreaming,
waiting,
ready for me to interrupt you,
eager to hear me remind you
that we are alive.

We are alive together.

So when I tell you, *I love you*
I mean it in the ways they do
on television and in books
(and inside the looks they give one another
across candlelit tables)
but more than that, I mean it
in all the ways I hadn't planned for—
the ways I now
can't imagine
living without.

I wanted to finish something I started
so I started with you.

Shapes

My favorite shape
is the circle of your arms
around the cylinder of my waist.

The exclusion of space.

That Woman

I want to be that woman for you

a subtle cedar
with roots so deep
they make contact with your thirst zone
and neither weary
nor recoil
at your need for drink.

I want to be patient
when it rains,
able to survive
the occasional downpour.

When I grow
I want the movement
to pull your soil
closer to the sun.

I want to be a safe sighing-ground,
brave enough
to hold the punching bag
and trusting enough to
let you swing.

I want to refrain from
burden-swapping
when you really need
to just unburden.

I want to give you silence and
head-nods
instead of a game plan,
a hand-massage instead of
defending the other team.

I wanna' stop talking
when I should be listening.

I want to give you
anything

but cyclone guilting
or another item
to add to "the list."

I want to give you a drink.
I will mix it for you,
help bring the glass to your lips
or your lips to my lips
or leave you alone,
whatever it is
you need.

I want to embody
peace
and empathy
and silence
and trust
and reminders
of God

without saying a word.

But I know
that I won't
always be
that woman.

I just need you to know that I want to be.

Sand Tiger Shark

Your spirit animal is a
sand tiger shark.
I know because you
don't flinch when someone cries and
seem uncomfortable meeting eyes, you
eat your meals alone, were
born having already grown
hardened,
defensive
and sick, it's
as if you came out fighting to
prove your worth by biting the
heads off each of your sisters,
their brothers, your brothers,
now dead inside you, fed
the energy to swim,
to breathe,
to live,
now

the ocean swallows you,
the way you swallowed them.

She Matters

She used to warm the IV bag
before connecting it to the tube
that ran through my veins
and into my heart.
She would
take my medicine out of the fridge,
hold it under her shirt, against her skin,
absorbing the piercing cold
so that I
didn't have to.
So that when
it raced up my arm
it would match the temperature of my blood.

And when I was still cradled inside of her,
attached like a pick line to her heart,
she would absorb each shiver,
sigh,
and pang
before it hit me.

At 17,
when the pain overwhelmed my body
her jaw became concrete.
Look at my daughter
she ordered the doctor.
She is not ok.
Do something.
Now.
And he did,
because my mother's words produce
orchards of results.
They do not return to her
without the discounted sweater,
the correct directions,
or the MRI that would reveal my crumbling spine.

She is a fixer,
and sometimes the only tool
that works on me these days
is packing tape—

care packages
containing house socks,
a new sweatshirt,
bamboo scented candles,
pop rocks,
and the book she "borrowed" from me
the last time I visited.

The truth is,
she is faithful
to steal every book
I am just about to read.
This is how she knows it's good.
I know it's good,
if she finishes it
and mails it back me.
We inhale good writing as if it were
the air at the coast,
sharp and fresh.
We exhale quotes
in the form of text messages to one another:
Talking to you makes my heavy boots lighter.
I read this message
before falling asleep.
She always writes when she is winding down
and I am turning in
because in California,
it's two hours earlier.

In the morning I wake up
to her 10 p.m. texts:
What should I watch on Netflix?
Peter the cat just tried to jump, but he's too fat now.
Luv you sweetie, goodnight.

And I know that when she hands her student
Brave New World
tomorrow and says: *You'll like this one,*
she's right.
He'll like it because she believes
that he is able

to understand great things

because she thought of him
when she picked it up,
the way she thinks about each person
as if they mattered most.

And I
am still learning
about all the ways that she matters.

Re-live

It was an August afternoon
when I heard the tip-toe sound
of something trying to end.

Our memories,
long placed on pause,
decided to stretch
and grasp
for the remote control
under my couch cushion.

That powerful remote
controlled
your presence in my life.

At my touch
the tape went fuzzy.
Black & white
bobbed under strobe lights.

I heard the splash and buzz
of a thousand interrupted scenes,
conversations,
feet next to each other on the coffee table,
blown kisses,
movie kisses,
hello-again kisses,
kisses that lacked zing,
kisses that meant everything;

late night moods that revealed our inner insanity,
connection
and our most embarrassing laugh.

I wanted to dive for those memories
collecting around my ankles like pools of water.
I wanted to chase the liquid of them
with a force
that would cause evaporation
to surrender.

But I couldn't.

For a moment
I saw everything clearly.

And the next moment
made it all disappear.

They Say

You can't beat that feeling
of concrete cold control,
a throat full
of swallowed emotions.

I gulp them down
when you're around;
drink baking soda with water
to break up the longing.

I guess I didn't know you.
I guess I didn't really know you.

Please close your shades.
Get a new muffler for your car.
Dust my chalk heart
off your summer driveway.

I Need to Get Away

I'm starving for a picnic
on the shore of a California beach;

a chance to relive those twelve-hour vacations
that were more than a day off work,
a day off school,
or a day to ditch
the daily grind.

They were
this-is-the-life moments
that got me through the rest of the year.

My dad's tennis shoes filling with sand,
bath towels posing as beach towels,
novels never to be read,
scattered around,
looking relaxing just lying there.
One of us setting off to find a shell
that isn't broken,
that is perfect and smooth.

I want to feel those memories
in the calm-me-down
content-with-this
part
of my stomach
while I let the sun make a color wheel
on the inside of my eyes.

Please

make me an uncomplicated sandwich

and spread it with peace
or peanut butter,
whichever is on hand.

Because
like a mermaid returning to sea-weed bed sheets
after a trial run with Egyptian cotton,

I am home again—
feeding off the waves
that fuel something inside me
that goes dry
when I've been away for too long.

Tell me with your eyes,
you-don't-have-to-go-back-just-yet.

Tell me,
that sunburn looks great on you.

Tell me that sand is nature's pedicure
and that when I take off my shoes
I become a world traveler,

standing on stones
that have touched a thousand shores.

Strangers

I.
I like the man in the coffee shop yesterday
who leaned over and confessed to me
I love coming here so much
I bring my laptop and surf the web
for information I don't need.
He grinned and lifted his cup
above his head
in an imaginary toast.

II.
I love the teenagers I saw
making out in the park
under that big oak tree,
the one with limbs like knotted ropes
and leaves as thin as sliced parmesan cheese,
because they could have been making out
somewhere else.

III.
I love the two mothers
pushing their twin strollers
side by side down the street,
on their way to the post office,
the grocery store
or the jungle gym,
finding time to be friends
post mommy-hood.

IV.
I love the husky neighbor kid
who walks his dog
right past my house
every day after school
because he listens to his mom
and he's shy in an obvious
and endearing sort of way.

V.
I love the man sitting on top
of the trash can,

eating his dinner
of pork and beans
that he got from the mission
down the street,
because he was kind to me
when he didn't have to be.
Instead
he chuckled
when I said hello
and smiled, genuinely,
when I told him I'd pray.
He said,
Pray for a cure.
I asked,
A cure for what?
He said,
Schizophrenia.

His name was Chris.

Teaching is Like Water

Have you ever seen a completely serene lake?
I have.
One made entirely of glass.
When the bell rings the glass breaks
and students trickle through my door
as though someone were ringing out a sponge full of
eagerness,
chip-on-my-shoulder,
brush-in-my-locker
hair styles
and sleepy smiles.
They welcome me
at high tide
with the splash of backpacks hitting the floor.
They pool around the chalk board to
answer the question of the week:
What is your pet peeve?
Girls puddle into various corners
balancing sloshing pitchers of news.
I watch as they soak my carpet
while attempting to pour every last drop
into the cupped palms of their peers.

The second bell rings.
I kick off my shoes and wade in,
Open your books, please
and just like that, we're out at sea,
watching a very old man
hold a line that cuts deeply into his hands.
He is tired and he talks to himself.
My students find this odd and laugh at him,
call him crazy,
and one girl admits: *I talk to myself too, sometimes.*
I hope he makes it back to shore.
What is even the point of this story?
My morning is salty.

I look at their faces as we read,
sinking when I see her completing a late math assignment
under her copy of *The Old Man and the Sea*,
floating again when I see the boy

who is underlining every other quote
and becoming a lifelong Hemingway fan.
I bob,
up and down,
until a tidal wave hits.

One student is drowning
in his need for attention.
He throws a pencil at a classmate, just missing her eye.
The entire class must tread water while I
swim toward the student who splashes loudest.
I hate watching their legs get tired
and their arms grow weary
from waiting.
They deserve better than this.
But just like a school of fish must shift
when one changes course
they stop reading,
look up,
watch,
wait
and hope
that the drowning boy will give up his act
so that we
can see
if the old man
ever made it back.

The Silent Hour

I have been up reading

for hours, maybe.

I find myself awake
at a time
that is considered
neither early morning
nor late night,

but merely
the time
of hollow stillness
and giant
clock sounds.

I look up from my book

and from the window
see rain-
fall
like paint drippings;
turning the grey asphalt
gold.

I too am in the midst
of a rain;
a time
when the ground chokes
with everything
it has been needing.

I need
living water.

I need
a cup
that overflows.

I need
this rain

to pour down
and drown
what needs drowning.

The Mixer

He pours concrete.
It's his job,
his art,
his livelihood.
So yes,
he's good at it.

He begins with the perfect mixture
of sand,
born from heavy rocks
shaved weightless.

He adds water
to the teenage gravel,
and stirs
(easily at first).

His grip hardens,
as the ingredients connect.

The mixture is slow
and heavy
but won't stick
until it meets cement.

He adds this element
with eagerness,
the way a painter mixes colors,

the way this sadness
slides down my throat.

He is an artist.

A mixer of dust
and permanence.

When he pours his concrete,
he pours a death sentence
onto anything growing
beneath.

I thought he came
to fix my sidewalk

until I saw that his mold
was in the shape of my chest.

I didn't scream,
say no
or move away
as he deftly filled my hollow
with hardness.

Now,
every limb feels nailed to the floor,
every word
damp from the sweat of trying
to articulate this pain.

Each breath
heavy-lifting,

each hope,
harder to stir.

Buddy Wakefield

I hugged Buddy Wakefield tonight.

We embraced before we spoke.

The way of poets
is rarely about chronology.

In fact
they often drive for miles in reverse
just to see
what the past looks like
once they've gotten past it.

And absolutely anything is ok
as long as it's real.

When I listened to his words tonight
I realized that not being ok
is about as real as it gets.

His arm went out
like the tide
preparing to pull in
a day's worth of stones
and bottle caps
but it was just me
and both my arms
were already around his neck.

I spoke into his ear, so the crowded room
wouldn't rob my message:

*I read your poems to my mom sometimes. In the morning. While she does
her hair. When I read them, she cries.*

He thanked me
with his eyes
and maybe
with his mouth
but the room
had swallowed up our words

and it didn't really matter anyway because I had his wide, bloodshot stare
and my recollection
of his performance thirty minutes earlier
where trembling
had been fashioned into one hell of a communication tool
and the common pause

just about destroyed me.

I know he's used to strangers huggin' him.

He's used to people like me
clinging to him
like the open wounds they are,
hoping
his words do more than just
wash the gravel from their cuts
and temporarily remove the pillow
from the bass drum
in their chest
but that
his words will actually turn their scars
into a secret language
that only the imperfect can understand.

They hope
the embrace will act as a bandage
made popular by its tagline:
You will not bleed to death.

I hugged Buddy Wakefield tonight.

And I know I'll never forget it,
the crowded room,
the chairs that creaked *amen,*
the cold drinks,
and his words

that made being understood
safe again.

A Hard Conversation

She shuffles over to me, squeezing her book,
chewing on her lip, and giving me that look.
She says,
May I ask you a question?
Of course.
I must have read it wrong.
She mumbles and I become alert.
Girl's can't...
Can't what?
It says...
Says what?

I recognize in her
the desire to hide,
see that despite it
she must look inside
another world, another life,
even if it hurts.

It says in here something about a girl...
Yes?
A girl being circumcised.
But that can't happen, right?
Well...
It only happens to boys, right?
She
opens her book and scans the page,
hoping to find some error.

Under flickering, iridescent lights,
I sigh and search for words—
the softest euphemisms
she's ever heard.
But I know what I should have said:

Some people value tradition over trust
and think that leaving a woman whole
will only make her lust
so
they shut her
up

and cut her
off
from pleasure
fullness
and
dignity.

Instead I said,
Have you taken anatomy?
Next year.
Then I'm not sure this is something
you'll want to hear.

What?
Because.
How?
With.
Why?
Fear.

And hate.

Catching Lizards in the Summer

Their scaly chests pump up and down
and I try to calm them
by holding still
and staying quiet.
I notice their eyes
begin to close
and I think, childishly,
that they are asleep
or at least
that they have finally relaxed.
But the tiny heart doesn't slow down.
Despite closed eyes,
I can feel its beat against my palm.

Did you expect me to stay
lizard-cold
in the shape of your hand?

Did you think my heart was excited
to be captured
then released?

Summer has taught me
that the safest place
is not rock tops
but between stone and earth,
hidden from flesh
and blood.

You left

now
it's time to buy
a weighted blanket

the kind
that
competes with my heaviness

and wins.

Books

My friend used to tell me
how he sleeps with books.
They pile up
under blankets and pillows
like a lazy library.
They begin to take over
his side of the bed.

Now I sleep with them too,
instead of with you.

Salinas

When you suddenly have to
start over
you end up Googling places
you never considered living before.
Salinas, California.

Maybe I just want to
touch the earth
Steinbeck wrote about
with twisted admiration
as if it was worth
staying,
digging,
and waiting for the drought to end.

Maybe it's the kind of dirt
that has fresh potato potential,
because of the small living things
underneath
that are willing to take shallow breaths
until the day they feel
water
trickle down their backs again.

Maybe there is life
under the cracked surface
of things.

Either way, the apartments are too expensive.

Un-Becoming My Husband

In my old room, at my parent's house
I picture you walk in and sit down on the bed.
For a moment it brings me so much relief,
the way you look at me
with an understanding
that doesn't have to be discussed.

I crave that quiet nod of knowing lately
when my shoes fill up with sand
if I think too far down the road.
Or when a note from you falls out of one of my books.
The last one was scribbled on a church bulletin
on one of those Sundays when you still went to church.
It said, *I wish I could give you so much more*
than I am currently able to.
And I don't know if I want to save it.
Another was cut from red paper
into the shape of a heart:
You are my love, it said. Says.
Unless I throw it away
so as to avoid becoming a hoarder
of expiration dates.

If you were really in my room right now,
it wouldn't play out like comfort.
You would walk in and feel you needed to talk,
to drown out other things,
like the memories we are still trying to suffocate
or the emotions we don't describe
because it wouldn't help.

You would stand there,
and I would want to draw close,
in safety
and that carefree spirit I could only feel with you.
But I would restrain myself.
I wouldn't hug you
because you are un-becoming my husband,
a process of reverse that has no rules,
a death that feels like unintentional suicide.

Picturing you here
with me
right now
is a ticket stub of a day dream,
a sad reminder
of how lonely this all is
and will be.

But God,
have mercy.

Hot Tea

Thank you for letting me
make you hot tea
every time I asked,
despite your aversion to grace.

The Stories We Stop Telling

Tonight
when everyone shared their proposal stories
I held mine close
but hidden
the way we hold our cell phones under our coats
when it rains.

In the kitchen
at your apartment,
with a ring pop
because the real ring
was still in the mail

and you couldn't wait
to marry me.

What We Know in Part

When we finally learn to find beauty in the broken
it becomes hard to walk away from shadows,
dull mirrors
and the sad boys
who hold us in their arms.

We glue together all the parts
of what we *know in part*
hoping to form something
whole
in the right-now,
here-on-earth.

This hole demonstrates
our lack of wholeness.
This hole
is empty
like the tomb you left
to fulfill all your promises.

Was it cold that morning?
Did you feel some warmth from heaven
on your back?
Some excitement-shivers
at the thought
that you would be home soon?

Song of Experience

You were scared, so you called me.
They shot him on your front porch.
He stumbled into your house
held his head and bled all over your floor.
Don't tell mom.
I won't.
You don't call to tell me
about how you got beat up in Vegas.
I don't call to tell you
how worried I am.
Instead we talk
about the songs you're composing,
the stories I'm writing,
the summers we spent
walking barefoot over rocks,
building up calluses

so we wouldn't feel pain.

Hello, Doctor

If the doctors find
that there is water on my brain

I'll let it out myself

in streams
of consciousness.

If they diagnose me with
something as fragile-sounding
as a heart murmur

I'll put chin to chest and whisper,
*I kind of always thought
you were trying to tell me something.*

If it's arthritis
my hands will be the first to go
and I'll have to find a new way
to touch this generation.

If it's heart-burn
I'll give up steak
and replace tough chewing
with the calm coating
of feeding ducks on the shore at dusk.

And if it turns out its cancer,
I will beat it bloody
then check to make sure
it didn't survive.

But if the doctor calls me
into his office
and shakes his head,
strangles his pen
letting the creases run deep across his forehead

I'll know
it's something more fatal
something that cannot be fixed

and I'll lie awake
and smile (faintly)
at the realization that this
might be the best excuse
I've ever had

to live.

Rachel Joy Watson grew up in a small town in northern California, wearing overalls, playing outside, searching for bugs and getting sunburned ritualistically. After receiving her B.A. in writing and studying at Oxford for a summer, she began teaching high school English and has spent the last eight years trying to motivate her students to write and read bravely, always looking for connections between life and literature. She writes devotionally, paints her joy, and processes disenchantment, grief and courage through poetry.

She has had poems published in *Cordella Magazine* and occasionally contributes articles on theology and faith to *RELEVANT* and *The Gospel Coalition*. She is currently working on a Master of Letters in Bible and the Contemporary World from The University of St. Andrews and has an insatiable longing for salty ocean air.

CPSIA information can be obtained
at www.ICGtesting.com
Printed in the USA
LVOW10s1938190417
531397LV00010BA/1208/P